In this series –

RUMI READINGS
FOR
GRIEVING

RUMI READINGS
FOR
GRIEVING

JALALUDDIN RUMI

The Scheherazade Foundation

The Scheherazade Foundation CIC
85 Great Portland Street
London
W1W 7LT
United Kingdom
www.SF.Charity
info@SF.Charity

First published by The Scheherazade Foundation CIC, 2025

RUMI READINGS FOR GRIEVING

© The Scheherazade Foundation

The Scheherazade Foundation asserts the right to be identified as the Author
of the Work in accordance with the Copyright, Designs and Patents Act 1988.

A CIP catalogue record for this title is available from the British Library.

ISBN 978-1-915311-72-6

Introduction

Jalaluddin Rumi was born in Balkh, Afghanistan, in the year 1207, and died in Konya, Turkey, in 1273.

During the sixty-six years spanning this pair of dates, he produced a range of extraordinary work in Persian which, today, is classed as 'Sufi Mysticism'.

In the seven and a half centuries since his death, Rumi's corpus, which includes *The Masnavi* and *Fihi Ma Fihi*, has been circulated widely across the Near East, the Arab world, and Central Asia.

Generations of students continue to commit selections of the 60,000 verses to heart, and allow Rumi's way of thought to permeate through all areas of their lives.

Although Orientalists venturing eastward from Europe in the 1700s occasionally made note of Sufi Mysticism, they tended to witness it through the more theatrical frills – such as 'whirling dervishes' – rather than through a deep appreciation of the texts.

It wasn't until the close of the nineteenth century that the first wholescale translations of Rumi's written work began to appear in Europe.

Even then, they remained very much the purview of a few academics, whose translations were – even for the time – laden with indescribably floral and cumbersome prose.

Although in the Occident, students would find themselves scrutinizing Rumi's corpus, it wasn't until more recently that accessible appreciations of his work became available.

A few years before his death, I asked my father – the Sufi scholar and thinker Idries Shah – for his thoughts on Rumi's legacy in the West.

Sitting in his favourite chair, a porcelain cup of green tea in hand, he looked at me hard.

'I never cease to be amazed,' he said.

'Amazed by what?'

'By the way people don't take what's perfectly packaged, and ready and waiting for them, but rather obsess with something else.'

'With what?'

'With endless and nonsensical trimmings, trappings, and paraphernalia.'

My father sipped his tea.

After a moment of silent thought, he continued:

'Read Rumi in the original Persian,' he said, 'and so delicate are the verses that you have tears rolling down your cheeks. Yet here in the West, it's served up as something submerged in a thick, glutinous gravy, so much so that its utterly inedible.'

I reminded my father that a series of publications had recently found their way to press – publications that presented Rumi's couplets in an utterly new way.

Stripped bare of what my father had referred to as 'gravy', they were light.

Indeed, they were lighter than light.

My father rolled his eyes at the thought.

'In any other place, and at any other time,' he said, 'people would be up in arms. Or, if they weren't, they'd be laughing until their sides split. Imagine it – Western poets with absolutely no knowledge of the original Persian text touting new, bestselling editions of Rumi's work! It's what we call "The Soup of the Soup of the Soup".'

In the years since my father's death, Occidental society has been flooded with all things Rumi.

Couplets ascribed to him are read solemnly at weddings across the United States, Europe, and beyond.

Wisdom drawn from his poetry is tattooed daily over the backs and limbs of Hollywood A-listers.

But the precious words uttered at weddings, tattooed into skin, and quoted in abundance, hold little or no bearing to the original verses of Jalaluddin Rumi.

So, there it is…

The great Sufi Master's wisdom available:

(a) in a form that's unreadable because it's all covered in glutinous gravy, or

(b) in another form that's completely distorted – the Soup of the Soup of the Soup.

One thing that *is* evident is that the West can benefit enormously from a clean, clear rendition of Rumi's thinking – as the East has done over the last seven hundred years.

For this reason, we have commissioned entirely new translations, gleaned in particular from *The Masnavi*. Selected and translated by native Persian-speaking scholars, the emphasis has been on maintaining the lightness of Rumi's poetry.

In an age of relentless speed and digital overload, and so as to allow the work to be accessed by those who may benefit from it most, we have arranged a series of bite-sized morsels by way of theme.

We encourage you to do what students, scholars, and ordinary people have done across the East for centuries...

To pick a single couplet, or a handful – and to read them over and over, allowing them to seed themselves in your mind.

Little by little, having taken root, they will blossom and bear fruit.

Tahir Shah

How to Use This Book

Rumi Readings for Grieving

There is no map for grief.

No right pace, no clear path, no single way forward.

Grief arrives differently for everyone – as silence, as sobbing, as rage, as numbness, as love.

This book is not here to tell you how to grieve.

It is here to sit beside you while you do.

Rumi Readings for Grieving brings together one hundred passages drawn from the original Persian writings of Jalaluddin Rumi – selected largely from *The Masnavi* and translated afresh by The Scheherazade Foundation. These are not interpretations or approximations. They are faithful transmissions of a voice that has comforted hearts for centuries.

These verses are offered as companions in a time when words often fall short.

They do not attempt to explain away loss.

They do not ask you to move on.

They invite you to sit, to breathe, and to feel what is yours to feel.

Let this book be a quiet space where your sorrow is not rushed, not minimized – but met.

There Is No Correct Way to Use This

You can begin at the start, or open it at random.

You can read a quote every day, or once a week, or only when the wave of grief rolls highest.

If all you do is read a single line and feel less alone – that is enough.

The quotes are arranged in ten thematic parts – exploring the nature of death, the wisdom that grief can carry, the transformation of loss, and the paradox of love enduring beyond death.

But you are not required to follow that order.
You are not required to finish anything.

Grief has its own rhythm. Let the book meet you there.

Let the Words Work Slowly

You may not always understand the quotes right away. Some may seem obscure, or too sharp, or too gentle. Some may say just what you needed. Others may say nothing at all.

That's okay. This is not a puzzle to solve.

Let the words sit with you, like a candle lit in a dark room.
You don't have to stare at it. You don't even have to speak.
Just let the light be there.

Breathe With the Quote

When you find a line that speaks to your sorrow – or even touches something you can't quite name – try this:

- Read it slowly, out loud if you can.
- Sit with it in silence.
- Close your eyes. Notice how your body responds.
- Place your hand over your heart, or on your chest, and simply breathe.

This is not performance. This is presence. This is grief becoming sacred.

When You Need to Speak

Sometimes you may want to talk back to the quote – to argue with it, to cry into it, to tell your own story beside it. That's welcome.

Keep a notebook if you like. You may wish to write what the quote brings up in you – not neatly, not perfectly, but honestly.

There is no pressure.

Share It, If It Helps

You may find that one quote in particular speaks to what you cannot say. You might share it at a memorial. Or send it to a friend who is grieving. Or write it down and carry it in your pocket.

Rumi's words have long been used to say the unsayable. Let them speak when you cannot.

No Need to 'Feel Better'

This book does not aim to lift you out of grief. It does not offer solutions or silver linings.

It respects grief for what it is: a sacred, painful, transformative part of being human.

But it may offer company. It may soften a hard edge.

It may remind you that what you feel is not only valid – it is shared across time, by all who have ever loved and lost.

Rumi writes in this volume:

'Die, then, that you may arise from the eternal Essence. For from this death, a genuine life will be born.'

Whatever you are feeling – let it be enough.

Whatever you are carrying – let this book help carry it, even a little.

There is no rush.

There is no failure.

There is only the next breath.

Part 1
The Nature of Death

1

We have resided in the celestial realm, allies of the divine;
we shall return, for that is our true abode.

2

I witnessed death upon my emergence from you;
detachment from you was pain.
Upon my birth, I emerged from a confined existence
into a realm of vibrant and exhilarating atmosphere.
I perceived the universe as a womb until this moment,
when, amidst the flames, I saw tranquility.
In this conflagration, I perceived a realm,
each particle like the breath of Jesus.

3

All assert beauty and elegance,
yet the stone of death challenges the truth of
such assertions.

4

No one dies with remorse about dying itself;
their sole lament is that death arrived too soon.
They descended from a well into expansive plains
amidst prosperity, joy and contentment.

5

This body possesses no value to me.
In its absence, I am a youthful warrior,
progeny of the brave.
The dagger and sword transformed into blooms;
my death became a celebration, and a garden of narcissi.

6

He dismantled it to reconstruct it more effectively,
for the populace was magnificent,
yet their dwelling was inadequate.

7

One day, the Prophet visited the cemetery
at the funeral of a companion.
He filled the grave with soil,
and beneath the earth
his seed was rejuvenated.

8

Die without fear,
for from this terrestrial realm
you shall rise to the celestial.

9

Die, die, and liberate yourself from this breath,
for this breath is like a chain,
and you, its captives.
Use a hammer to beat into the cavity of your confinement;
upon the prison's collapse,
all shall rejoice and be liberated.

10

Death is perpetual union.
What is its nature?
It is God, the Singular.
Those who dwell in the illumination of God
find solace
in the demise of this spirit.

Part 2
The Multiplicity of Death

11

Each minute signifies death and rebirth.
The Prophet said:
'This world is but a moment.'
With every breath, both we and the universe
are made young again,
oblivious to our transformation within constancy.

12

The wave has arrived;
the vessel of form is constrained.
When the vessel fractures,
it is time for reunion and assembly.
'Alast': the Divine Word;
'Ship of Form': the corporeal vessel.

13

Die before your death;
for after death, riches shall come.
No other civilization can attain divinity,
O deceiver!

14

Numerous souls,
esteemed martyrs
existing in this realm,
yet moving along as
though already dead.

15

Life is obscured by the facade of death,
and death is embedded within the core of life.

16

Not a death confined to the grave,
but one that manifests in illumination.
Dust transforms into gold;
bodily form dissipates;
sorrow is replaced by pleasure;
the anguish of sadness ceases to exist.

17

The dead are united in a village,
succumbing to adversity;
Sufis have surrendered from a multitude of directions.
Death constitutes a singular act of killing;
yet this multitude entails an incalculable
cost of blood for each one.

18

The soul frequently remains asleep behind a shroud,
as you have yet to unveil the authentic nature of death.
Until there is death, the complete spirit cannot manifest;
without wholeness, ascension to greatness is unattainable.

19

As you extract life from the dead,
the dead undergo a transformation.
The living might develop from the dead
while the living soul hastens towards a form of death.
Die, then, that you may arise from the eternal Essence.
For from this death, a genuine life will be born.

20

True existence is found in death and hardship;
the essence of life lies hidden in mystery.

Part 3
The Wisdom of Death

21

You ignore what is unseen,
but mortality will soon clarify
your understanding.

22

His hidden kindness lies within His wrath;
surrendering your life to Him will elevate your soul.
Abandon doubt and deceit;
move forward, for He has called you to ascend.

23

If the incense within you ignites,
the universe will be filled with gentle fragrance.
You are neither the incense consumed by flames
nor the spirit trapped by sorrow.
Incense ignites through separation from the flame,
yet the wind cannot alter the essence of light.

24

Within creation there are pure souls
and those tainted by worldly impurities.
These shells differ in value;
one may hold a precious pearl,
while another contains a worthless stone.
It is crucial to separate the virtuous from the wicked,
as wheat is separated from the chaff.

25

All that we have observed thus far is only a glimpse.
This world is an illusion;
the next world holds the true essence.
The day of death is shrouded in mystery;
the seed is planted in the earth.
On leaving, the day of harvest comes;
the day of recompense arrives, and truth is unveiled.

26

He asked,
'What wisdom lies in life and its mysteries
when the pure essence is confined in this shadowy realm?'
Clear water is hidden in the mud;
the pure soul is trapped within bodily form.

27

Nothing is more bitter than separation from You;
there is no refuge except in You,
O Most Complex One.

28

O youth,
the emblem of genuine trust has manifested:
he who approaches you brings a serene death.
If your faith is lacking,
O soul,
then strive to enhance your faith.

29

Love transmutes lifeless matter into vitality,
and the annihilated soul attains eternity.

30

Injustice and benevolence, anguish and elation
are all ephemeral;
ephemeral entities fade,
and their essence belongs to the Eternal.

Part 4

On the Characteristics of One Who Experiences Death Before Dying

31

Attend to the narrative of the travellers
who harbour no objections in this world.

32

Life is not for oneself,
nor for savouring the delightful essence of existence.
Wherever a command exists, a path follows;
for them, life and death are indistinguishable.

33

They exist for the divine, not for wealth;
they die for the divine,
not out of fear of pain.

34

Why does he implore through prayer,
'O God, avert this disaster!'?

35

The prayer is valid due to his annihilation;
both the prayer and its realization originate from God.

36

No lover desires to unite with himself,
for he does not yearn for his Beloved.

37

The torment of his qualities is love,
and he has incinerated each trait individually.

38

They ridicule death,
which instills terror in them.

39

As I have died before my natural death,
I have conveyed this resonance from beyond.
Therefore, awaken to the Day of Judgement and observe it;
perceiving anything necessitates this condition.

40

A servant possessing such qualities and characteristics would command the world's obedience.

Part 5
Fear or Fearlessness of Death

41

O son,
each person's death reflects their true essence:
to the enemy, it is an enemy;
and to the friend, it is a friend.
What you fear as death rising above
is merely your fear of yourself.
Be aware, O soul.

42

False intelligence sees things the wrong way around:
it views life as death,
O deluded one!
May God reveal all things as they genuinely are
in this deceiving realm of existence.

43

Those who live indulgently will meet a painful end;
those who venerate the corporeal will not redeem the spirit.

44

If any aspect of death appears pleasant to you,
understand that it is God
who makes its entirety sweet.
The pangs serve as heralds of death;
do not disregard His envoy,
O foolish one!

45

Do not bid me adieu as you bury me,
for the tomb is but a shroud of assembly.
As the sun sets, observe the ascent;
why should the sunset
and its fading light be wept over?

46

When the universe is besieged and confined,
what astonishment is there
if the suffering individual is ephemeral?

47

Recognize that all suffering is an aspect of mortality;
   if a cure exists, eliminate the element of death.
   As you cannot evade the inevitability of death,
understand that it will ultimately descend upon you.

48

Those who consume the wine of death are sustained
by love; they have detached their hearts
from the soul and the essence of life.
Upon the arrival of love's essence,
the significance of the water of life
diminishes in our presence.

49

Romantic partners experience death at every moment;
and a lover's death manifests in several forms.
He possesses two hundred souls from
the essence of guidance,
and he continuously sacrifices these two hundred.

50

Do not hesitate to move forwards,
for death is a wolf,
and your spirit a sheep.
Should you transform into the immortal and divine lion,
rest assured that your demise
will be filled with sweetness.

Part 6
Neglect or Awareness
of Death

51

The negligent resemble snow-capped mountains
preventing the wise from burning their veils.
Were it not for the veil of ignorance obscuring the snow,
Mount Qaf[1] would have been consumed
by the flames of desire.

---

1   A legendary mountain in Middle Eastern tradition.

52

Negligence can sometimes be viewed as both
prudence and a blessing,
ensuring that one's assets are not quickly forfeited.

53

If people could perceive their own shortcomings,
how would they neglect the imperative
for self-improvement?
They are oblivious to their own flaws,
which is why they always highlight
the deficiencies of others.

54

'Do not hold us accountable if we forget,'
serves as evidence that,
in some regard,
forgetfulness may also constitute a sin.

55

The soul elevates you towards the celestial realms,
yet you have plunged the depths
towards the earth and soil.

56

A life devoid of repentance is perpetual suffering;
death looms while one remains detached from reality.

57

As you are my entirety,
why do you detach a part from the whole?
When a component is separated from the totality,
it becomes ineffective;
when a limb is amputated from the body,
it becomes inanimate.

58

With you, there is life and vigour;
without you, there is deterioration and death,
for you are the sun,
and in your absence, we are inactive.

59

I have discovered that my death is
intertwined with existence,
as my journey to eternity traverses this life.

60

Similar to the world, which is truly a transient illusion,
it perceives itself as eternal during its sleep.
Suddenly, the onset of death emerges,
liberating us from the shadows of doubt and deception.

Part 7
The Nature of Emotion in the Encounter With Death

61

The unsuspecting bird consumes
the bait from the trap,
as people are ensnared
by the allurements of the world.

62

We were once parrots that articulated delightful notions,
but thanks to your influence
we have transformed into birds preoccupied with death.

63

Our moon is not obscured by clouds:
for us there is no harshness of darkest night;
death is nonexistent for lovers,
allowing us to evade its grief.

64

How can it be painful for a person to be removed from the poison of serpents to the sweetness of sugar?

65

Do not speak,
for only those in need of expression should articulate.
Pursue the quintessence of discourse,
for it is of paramount importance.

66

Our forebears, the four elements, are primordial;
we, through appropriated greed,
have asserted a connection with them.

67

What constitutes the ascension of the heavens?
It is nonexistence; for lovers,
the doctrine and belief are nonexistence.

68

The body is inevitably destined to decay,
yet the essence shall endure in perpetual bliss.

69

This absence represents an opportunity for wealth;
this existence signifies a realm of expense,
regardless of the amount.

70

In the workshop of Your affection,
devoid of You,
whatever I create – by God,
not a single thread endures, nor filament.

Part 8
Death & Life

71

Understanding that death
encompasses numerous gardens
would lead you to discover eternal life
in the perpetual quest for the soul.

72

Its face conveys death,
yet its core embodies life;
its outer form may appear desolate,
yet concealed within is permanence.

73

The night is extinguished and revives;
existence persists beyond death.
O grief, embrace me within you.

74

For those whose existence is intertwined with love,
there is no death; do not assume
that annihilation awaits them.

75

I embraced austerity and piety as my beliefs,
as I perceived death looming ahead.
Death has become my neighbour,
a harbinger to me,
interrupting my enterprise and
my establishment.

76

When aversion dissipates,
it is not death itself;
it is rather the semblance of death,
a transition to be navigated.
When aversion dissipates,
death becomes advantageous,
being evident that death is, in fact, a benefit.

77

Recognize that each pain signifies a fragment of mortality;
if possible, expel that aspect of death from within yourself.
As you cannot evade a part of death,
understand that its fullness will ultimately come
if a sample of death is pleasurable to you.

78

Similar to a candle's flame in the presence of the sun,
it appears insignificant, yet holds value.
It exists; yet, when cotton is placed against it,
it ignites and vanishes.

79

I experienced death and returned,
having encountered the sharpness of
mortality and non-being.

80

Relief follows adversity; do not lose hope.
You possess a path from death to existence.

Part 9

The Quality of True Life and Death

81

If not externally in the grave,
it is even lower; graves have overtaken his senses.
You have seen the dead in the tomb;
now see the dead within the grave of aspirations,
O blind ones!

82

Return to the mine once more
and extract only pure gold
to cleanse your hands of impurities.

83

They are perpetually aged and decrepit,
for when the previous moment occurs, it is revitalized.
It revitalizes the long dead,
granting the diadem of reason and
the illumination of belief.

84

What essence can you transform into words?
The truth invigorates you with His affection.
Seek existence through love,
and refrain from looking for the spirit;
ask Him for nourishment beyond ordinary bread.

85

Restricted like a plant in the soil,
you yield to a gust of uncertainty.
Yet you possess no feet on which to depart.
Perhaps you should free your feet from the dirt.

86

When one mouth closes,
another opens,
absorbing fragments of hidden truths.
By freeing the body from the devil's nourishment,
you will reap abundantly from divine blessings.

87

Upon spiritual rebirth,
the individual rises to the pinnacle of causation.

88

A change in disposition is necessary,
for death stems from a harmful temperament.
When a person's nature becomes indulgent,
they grow pale, weak, and unwell.
But when their unpleasant nature transforms,
the unattractiveness fades from their face,
and they shine, radiant like a candle.

89

They are dead and decayed through destruction;
it is not our task to finish what is already lifeless.
Who are they, that even the moon should split for them
when I press my foot firmly in the conflict?

90

Though the days may pass, say:
'Depart, it matters not.'
For you endure, O pure being,
beyond all comparison.

Part 10

Meeting with
the Messenger of Death

91

Will your current perception vanish
on the day of death?
Do you possess a radiance of spirit
that can accompany your heart?

92

Upon death, his pain dissipates;
he is consumed by it as the soul departs.

93

The death of the physical form is a blessing
for the preservation of secrets;
what harm can befall untainted gold?

94

People in the marketplace may share a similar gait,
yet one expresses joy while the other suffers.

95

Death is burdensome for the souls of the heedless,
as they lack the eternal essence of the spirit.

96

He said:
'I will elucidate the methods distinctly
through fever, cramps, delirium, and afflictions,
to divert their attention from you
through interconnected ailments and causes.'

97

He whose ultimate resting place is but
a small quantity of dust,
what necessity exists to elevate a castle to the heavens?

98

The Prophet said:
'On this journey,
no companion is more faithful than one's actions.
If they are virtuous,
they will be your everlasting companion;
if they are malevolent,
they will become your affliction after death.'

99

Fortunate is the one who evades this domain,
for death is the annihilator of this realm.

100

What you intend to express at my burial,
articulate it now; do not abandon
my despondent spirit unredeemed.

Finis

www.ingramcontent.com/pod-product-compliance
Lightning Source LLC
Chambersburg PA
CBHW020450100426
42813CB00031B/3317/J